Original title:
Fiddle-Leaf Futures

Copyright © 2025 Creative Arts Management OÜ
All rights reserved.

Author: Matthew Whitaker
ISBN HARDBACK: 978-1-80581-832-8
ISBN PAPERBACK: 978-1-80581-359-0
ISBN EBOOK: 978-1-80581-832-8

Alive in Shadows

In corners where the light can't creep,
A leafy friend begins to leap.
With laughter hiding in their veins,
They dance around like playful chains.

Their leaves conspire and hold a grin,
Whispers of joy amidst the din.
Who knew green could be so spry?
A leafy prankster, oh my, oh my!

Thriving Dreams

In pots of clay they scheme and sway,
Dreams of sunshine come out to play.
With roots that wiggle and stretch out wide,
They giggle softly, oh what a ride!

While humans fret and count the cost,
These greens are found, never lost.
Chasing dreams with every sprout,
In a game where fun's the clout!

Radiant Blooms of Tomorrow's Canvas

With paints of green and strokes of cheer,
They craft a world that's truly dear.
Petals popping with a wink,
A riot of colors, don't you think?

Each bloom a canvas, bright and bold,
Crafting stories yet untold.
With laughter splashed in every hue,
They invite us in, a grand debut!

Green Gestures of Hopeful Echoes

In the dance of leaves, laughter swells,
Each rustle sings of hidden spells.
They whisper secrets to the air,
While mischief bounces everywhere!

With gestures green, they play their role,
Crafting joy from every hole.
Hope springs forth from tangled vines,
In silly dances, life aligns!

Spirals of Nature's Lively Breath

As the wind twirls with a sigh,
Leaves take flight and then comply.
They spin and laugh in wild delight,
A merry chase through day and night.

Whirling twigs and spiraled fronds,
Make jolly tunes with nature's bonds.
In every twist and every turn,
A lively breath, we laugh and learn!

Leafy Expressions of Time's Tapestry

In a pot where sunlight beams,
A leaf dreams of grander schemes.
It stretches out its emerald spree,
Wishing it could dance like a bee.

But here it sits, with roots so shy,
While friends around the garden die.
A gossip of the soil's delight,
The leaf just laughs and holds on tight.

Time ticks by, it rolls and spins,
The leaf just grins, it always wins.
With whispers cheap and chubby stems,
It mulls its life on leafy whims.

So let it grow, this silly sprout,
In every twist, it finds a route.
With every sunbeam, it'll proclaim,
Life's leafy dance is such a game!

Sunlit Promises in Urban Corners

In a crack of concrete, bold and bright,
A leafy hero claims its right.
With laughter as its blooming voice,
It makes the gray feel like a choice.

The sun bestows its golden wink,
While pedestrians stop to think.
"What's this green, in all this gloom?"
It giggles loud, "I'll find some room!"

A pigeon struts, a dog runs by,
The leaf looks up, lets out a sigh.
Yet in its heart, a joy does swell,
Urban life is treating it well.

With every gust, it shakes and sways,
A silly dance for city days.
Against the odds, it finds its charm,
Proving leafy dreams won't harm!

Nature's Pulse among the Avenues

On busy streets where life's a rush,
   A leafy being does not hush.
It taps its foot on pavement gray,
   And sings of nature in ballet.

With each honk, it sways in tune,
A leaf on break beneath the moon.
It waves at cars, with playful ease,
   Transforming stress into a breeze.

Sidewalks hum with bustling beat,
   Yet here's a leaf with light, discreet.
A tiny world wrapped up in green,
   Stirring laughter wherever seen.

So next time life feels out of turn,
   Look for the leaf, let joy return.
Among the concrete, life persists,
With leafy smiles that can't be missed!

Whispers of Life in Leafy Form

In the twilight, the leaves conspire,
To share secrets as they tire.
"Did you see that cat?" one leaf laughs,
"It tried to steal my ferny drafts!"

The wind chimes in with silly tales,
Of squirrels with nuts and clumsy fails.
They gossip about the garden scene,
A leafy league, all dressed in green.

With every swish, a joke unfurls,
As petals dance and laughter swirls.
In leafy form, they dream and scheme,
Life's punchlines echo like a dream.

So when you're down, just stop and hear,
What leafy whispers might appear.
For every leaf has tales to tell,
And funny laughs that mesh so well!

The Unfolding of Nature's Wishes

In a pot, a dream does curl,
Tiny leaves begin to twirl.
Wiggling branches, oh so spry,
Nature's wishes dancing high.

With a sip of morning dew,
They look around, 'What's new for you?'
Chatting leaves with playful glee,
Plotting tales of what could be.

Each leaf whispers, 'What a show!'
'Let's grow tall, and steal the glow!'
Sunshine giggles, quite impressed,
Nature's dreams are truly blessed.

In the garden, laughter flows,
A leafy band in greenish clothes.
With each sprout, a joke is born,
In this world, we are reborn.

Horizons Woven with Green

Under sky, there's mischief sown,
Clever roots have brightly grown.
Branches stretch and twist with pride,
Nature's whimsy, can't confide.

Silly squirrels make a fuss,
Dancing leaves, they just can't trust.
With a bounce, they claim the day,
'Where's the nut?' they laugh and sway.

A garden plot of hope and cheer,
With each bud, we'll hold them near.
Roots are tangled, but who cares?
Nature's joy is found in layers.

So join the fun, let's spread the cheer,
In a world where green is near.
With playful greens and sunny beams,
We'll weave our wildest, leafy dreams.

Cascade of Leaves and Whispers

In the breeze, the giggles fly,
Leaves are plotting, oh so sly.
Each fluttered joke, a sudden tease,
Nature's whispers in the trees.

Tiny sprouts joke about their height,
As they stretch toward the light.
'Why stand still?' the branches cry,
'Let's prance around, reach for the sky!'

With a rustle, secrets spread,
The rumors of a garden bed.
Roses blush, and daisies nod,
Nature laughs, a mighty god.

As colors spin in joyful dance,
A riot of green takes a chance.
In this canopy of quirky dreams,
Every leaf bursts at the seams.

Nature's Canvas of Tomorrow

Brushes of green paint the day,
Nature giggles in its play.
Canvases of quirks and laughs,
Sketching out the plants' half-crafts.

Each sprout dreams of being grand,
Giggling roots beneath the sand.
'We'll grow strong!' they cheer and boast,
In this garden, we'll raise a toast.

As petals blush and daisies grin,
Nature's mischief makes us spin.
Every branch a story told,
In this laughter, we are bold.

With each day, the palette glows,
In the garden, wonder flows.
Nature's canvas, wild and free,
Laughing leaves, a jubilee!

Tendrils Reaching for the Sky

In the corner, a leaf does sprout,
Swaying gently, there's no doubt.
Reaching high, it bends and twists,
Looks like a dancer, it insists.

Neighbors laugh at the odd show,
Their faces scrunched, they just don't know.
Green arms stretching, such a sight,
Waving hello, morning light.

What a sight, a leafy friend,
Silly growth that will not end.
On a mission to grow tall,
Climbing higher, defying all!

With every inch, it raises cheer,
Applause for each new frontier.
Not just a plant, a wild display,
A leafy rebel, come what may!

Canopies of Hope in Urban Spaces

Between asphalt and concrete grey,
A splash of green found its way.
Leaves high-five the passerby,
A little cheer beneath the sky.

Oh, the joy of urban greens,
Sprouting hope in urban scenes.
Bugs line up for coffee breaks,
Underneath those leafy flakes.

With each branch, dreams take flight,
Finding sunlight in the night.
Robins joke, "We live in style!"
Perched on leaves, they always smile.

City folks can't help but stare,
At the plants who just don't care.
They laugh, they play, and grow so bold,
In this jungle, life unfolds!

A Tangle of Growth and Light

In a pot, a twisty mess,
With leaves in a playful dress.
Grinning roots span out like jokes,
It's like the plant tells puns to folks.

A leafy crown, nobody knows,
If it's a plant or circus show.
Fingers reaching, aiming high,
Bouncing back like a rubber sky.

Caterpillars join the fun,
Swinging low, but on the run.
They munch and laugh, a hopping spree,
Who knew plants had company?

Light beams join the leafy dance,
Making every moment a chance.
What a tangle, oh so bright,
In this patch, it feels just right!

Roots of Resilient Aspirations

Beneath the soil, there's a party,
Roots are chatting, none too tardy.
Whispers churn with hopes and dreams,
In the dark, they plot their schemes.

They dig deep, they stretch and roam,
Finding ways to make a home.
Braving storms and sneaky bugs,
Who knew roots could share such hugs?

Each sprout is like an ancient sage,
Cracking jokes upon the stage.
"Keep it green and keep it fun,
We're not done, we've just begun!"

Amongst the dirt, a laugh rings clear,
Aspire high, shed a cheerful tear.
Resilient hearts beat underground,
In this earthy joy, so profound!

Germination of Untold Stories

In pots where secrets grow, a dance,
Tiny roots shake hands, take a chance.
Budding tales in sunbeams sprout,
Whispered giggles, there's no doubt.

Planting dreams in quirky soil,
Each seedling laughs, begins to toil.
With every leaf, hilarity spreads,
As fun unfolds, the garden treads.

Breathing Life into Still Spaces

In quiet corners, laughter roots,
Dust bunnies dance, in leafy suits.
Chlorophyll giggles fill the air,
As plants play tag, without a care.

Pots like hats, they wear with glee,
Spreading joy, as green can be.
Your coffee sips with side-eye glints,
While flowers prank and plot their hints.

Overseas Horizons of Young Leaves

Across the seas, the leaves are bold,
Tickling breezes with tales untold.
They wave goodbyes and send postcards,
From sunny fields with merry guards.

They dance on tides of stories vast,
With roots that travel, none are last.
Each leaf a traveler, quite absurd,
Spreading laughs with every word.

Growing Tomorrow's Reveries

In whimsical gardens, futures bloom,
With vines that chuckle and flowers that zoom.
Beneath the sun, the laughter grows,
In every bud, a joke bestows.

Leaves whisper secrets, green with jest,
As nature plans its playful quest.
Tomorrow's dreams in compost mold,
Adventures sprout, both bright and bold.

Green Horizons and Soft Sunbeams

In a pot so round, the green leaves dance,
Hoping for light and a sunny chance.
They stretch and sway in a funny ballet,
Dreaming of sunbeams to brighten their day.

Chasing the shadows, dodging the gloom,
In a quirky race to find some more room.
Their roots whisper gossip below the ground,
While above, silly ants march all around.

With a wink and a nod, they tease the breeze,
Demanding a tickle from playful trees.
Oh, the laughter in every sprouting bud,
As they sip on rain like it's the best of suds.

So here's to the greens in their sunny attire,
Growing their dreams, never to tire.
With every sprout, a giggle is born,
In the garden of joy, they spread out and adorn.

Tides of Growth in the Urban Jungle

Amidst the concrete, they wiggle and play,
Urban jungles where the strange vines sway.
With each new leaf, a story unfolds,
Of humor and growth that never gets old.

The taxis honk, but they just won't care,
With roots so deep, they'll take their own dare.
A breeze through the alley sends them in spins,
And in every twist, a giggle begins.

Fish out of water? Not quite their style,
They thrive on the hustle, grow taller with guile.
When raindrops plop, they do a quick dance,
In the city's sway, they're taking their chance.

So raise up a toast to the green and the spry,
With laughter and light, they'll always comply.
Each leaf a chuckle, each petal a grin,
In this tangled, wild world, let the fun begin!

Flourishing beneath the Canopy

Beneath the tall trees, they sip and delight,
Chasing their dreams through morning's soft light.
In the shade, they sing out a playful refrain,
While squirrels debate if to dance or to gain.

With a twist and a turn, it's life on a leaf,
In joyous communion, there's null for grief.
The sunbeams drop gently, a warm golden shower,
Inviting each sprout to claim their green power.

They giggle at clouds that bring drizzles and mists,
Underneath leafy arches, they share secret lists.
Of quirky adventures, and tales of the day,
Where fun is the currency, come laugh, come play!

With roots intertwined, and laughter aligned,
Every inch of earth, an oasis defined.
So here's to the greens, in the sun's warm embrace,
Beneath the great canopy, they flourish with grace.

Life's Green Mosaic Evolving

In patches of chaos, a mosaic takes shape,
Colors and textures, a quirky escape.
With laughter like rain that tickles their leaves,
In a web of green, all nature believes.

They spin silly stories in every lost nook,
Mischief and wonder on every sweet hook.
Luxuriating in sunshine, they strut and they sway,
Wishing all pineapples could root down in clay.

A car honks its horn—"Hey, stay in your lane!"
Yet they giggle aloud, dance a light-hearted game.
With every new sprout, they laugh as they grow,
In this vibrant mosaic, let the good times flow.

So toast to the greens with joy on their lips,
Each leaf a know-it-all, with funny quips.
In the grand scheme of life, in each twist and turn,
They teach us to giggle and always to learn.

Dreams Woven in Green

Leaves dance like they own the floor,
Whispering secrets, always wanting more.
A plant in the corner with a cheeky grin,
Plotting adventures, ready to begin.

Sunbeams sprinkle magic on every leaf,
A daily giggle, a silly belief.
You think it's just foliage, just sitting there,
But plot twist! It's planning a future affair.

Mapping the Flora of Tomorrow

Silly sprouts with a map in hand,
Charting a course through this wild land.
They giggle together, full of glee,
Imagining cities where green dreams flee.

Crayons and soil make the perfect pair,
Drawing leafy layouts with a flair.
Who knew a seed could have such plans?
Building jungles with tiny hands!

Resilient Green in a Concrete Jungle

In a world of gray, a green thumb shines,
Planting a party where sunshine aligns.
Every crack in the sidewalk, a dance floor grand,
Where nature's ballet takes a stand.

With gumption they sprout, laugh at the stone,
Claiming their space with a whimsical tone.
Grass has no worries, it knows how to sway,
The city can't stop it, come what may!

The Art of Natural Resilience

Watch the cacti wear their hats of pride,
Living their lives with spines as their guide.
They poke fun at flowers, oh what a sight,
"Come join our show, we're bold and bright!"

Bouncing back from storms, they stand quite tall,
"Who needs the rain? We can dance after all!"
A cactus can giggle, a fig can be sly,
Nature's a sketch that tickles the eye.

Palettes of Possibility and Green

In the corner, plants conspire,
With leaves like dreams that reach higher.
Messy arrangements, oh what a sight,
Growing chaos in the morning light.

Sprouting hopes in pots so round,
Every leaf is a giggle, so profound.
Water spills with a playful splash,
A botanical dance, a leafy bash!

Sisters, brothers, roots intertwined,
In this botanical family, joy is aligned.
Thriving greens, a mischievous crew,
Catching laughs as they stretch anew.

Toast to the plants, in their leafy domain,
Whispering secrets that keep us sane.
In this quirky garden, we'll sway and sing,
With every shoot, let the laughter ring!

Kaleidoscope of Shades and Dreams

In the corners where shadows play,
Tiny plants dream of a bright ballet.
A patchwork of greens, so eager to grow,
Twirling in fun with the sun's warm glow.

Each leaf a joke, with laughter in tow,
Cracking whispers when breezes blow.
Their vibrant hues like a painter's brush,
In this green gallery, we all feel the rush.

Dancing pots will sway and spin,
As houseplants plot how to begin.
Giggling to themselves over dirt and toil,
Each little sprout delights in the soil.

What a scene, oh what a glee,
In the world of chlorophyll, wild and free!
Let's toast mocktails to these greens, so bold,
In this kaleidoscope, laughter unfolds!

Visions in Verdant Embrace

In this room where green dreams gather,
Plants wear smiles; oh what a blather!
Peeking leaves in a sunlight dance,
Swaying gently, taking a chance.

Ferns laugh softly, sharing a tale,
Of a past where they once set sail.
In pots decorated with whimsy and cheer,
A verdant embrace makes worries disappear!

A botanical circus under the sun,
Bringing joy, oh what fun!
I watch them grow, as they twist and shout,
In their green jubilation, they flail about.

In these visions of leaves and delight,
They promise joy, each day, each night.
So raise your cups to this merry crew,
In their verdant embrace, life feels brand new!

Sprouting Possibilities in Warm Light

In warm sunshine, they reach for the sky,
Little green warriors, oh my, oh my!
Roots tangled like silly socks,
Sprouting dreams in their cozy pots.

Buds winking, with mischief in tow,
As if they're painting a vibrant show.
Hilarity bubbles with every new leaf,
In this garden of joy, they're masters of belief.

Plants with character, each unique charm,
Growing tales of warmth, never harm.
In soft light, they shimmer and shine,
Sprouting possibilities, oh how divine!

So join the parade of green delight,
With laughter and sunshine, it feels so right!
Let's toast to the whims of our leafy friends,
In warm light, where all laughter blends!

The Poetry of Botanical Resilience

In pots of green, they stand so tall,
Their leaves defy the garden's brawl.
With sun and water, they just thrive,
A leafy dance, so fun and alive.

While other plants just throw a fit,
These leafy champs won't ever quit.
In storms they sway, and rocks they munch,
With roots like ninjas, they pack a punch.

A sprinkle here, a dance of light,
They shimmy close, full of delight.
In nature's play, they find their groove,
With every leaf, they bust a move.

So here's to greens that joke and jest,
Through ups and downs, they love the quest.
In every crack, they find a chance,
All while doing a leafy dance!

Nature's Secret Garden of Hope

Beneath the sun, they plot and scheme,
Planting joys like a silly dream.
With laughter ringing through the leaves,
They tickle roots and play tricks on bees.

In hidden spots, they share a jest,
A garden full of leafy zest.
With whispers soft, they tell their tale,
Of secret heights and leafy trail.

A twist of vine, a cheeky sprout,
Who says that gardens must be stout?
They giggle gleefully with each breeze,
These playful greens, they aim to please!

So let the world just try to frown,
In this green haven, joy's renown.
With every stem and every bloom,
Laughter erupts, dispelling gloom!

Blossoms of Tomorrow's Dreams

Pick a petal, spin a tale,
Whisper dreams with a leafy sail.
They plot out futures, bright and clear,
With giggles sprouting, full of cheer.

Each bud a secret, each leaf a laugh,
In this green world, there's no gaff.
A blossom here, a chuckle there,
They sprout designs beyond compare!

Tomorrow's blooms all dressed in jest,
A funny garden, simply the best.
With colors splashed like silly art,
These quirky greens all play their part.

So let your heart take root and grow,
Among the laughter, let it flow.
In gardens bright with joy and light,
Tomorrow's dreams are in full flight!

Leafy Reveries in the Breeze

Rustling whispers, a breezy chat,
Leaves tell secrets, like an old cat.
With every twirl, they dance and tease,
In leafy reveries, they find their ease.

A tickle from the wind goes round,
Each frond a story, joy abound.
They sway to rhythms, funny and bold,
In this leaf circus, wonders unfold.

Sprout a giggle, or two, or three,
Nature's jesters, wild and free.
In swirls of green, they make their scene,
A comedy club in between the greens.

So join the fun, let laughter bloom,
In nature's arms, dispelling gloom.
With every rustle, a joke is spun,
In leafy delight, there's always fun!

A Tapestry of Green Aspirations

In pots of dreams, they sway and bend,
Hoping the light will be their friend.
They fashion thoughts from every beam,
A leafy choir, a sunny dream.

With roots entwined, they plot and scheme,
Whispers of growth, a leafy team.
They tickle the air with flirty glee,
Dancing leaves, come waltz with me!

Sipping water like morning tea,
Little green folks, so carefree.
In a jungle made of yarn and thread,
They laugh at worries and dance instead.

A tale of joy, no need to fret,
In a home where green's the safest bet.
With each new sprout, come tales anew,
In their verdant world, they'll always bloom!

Echoing Life in Every Leaf

Laughter rustles in emerald veins,
Each leaf chuckling at life's refrains.
Breezy whispers, giggles without end,
In chlorophyll laughter, we all blend.

With every twist and wobbly sway,
They plan escapes to sunny bays.
Twirling in clouds of comforting light,
In their green kingdom, all feels right.

Giggling roots and a jittery stem,
They hold a ball, inviting them.
Windy dances on the living room floor,
A party of plants, who could want more?

Symphonies sung by the stalks at noon,
Beneath the watchful gaze of the moon.
Every leaf, a story to tell,
In their vibrant world, all is swell!

The Pulse of Natural Whispers

With every breeze, a playful nudge,
A secret giggle, a leafy grudge.
They pulse and flutter in joyful sync,
In emerald whispers, they start to think.

Fluffy clouds and plastic string,
They plot adventures fit for a king.
Letting sunlight in for a cheeky grin,
A green carnival, let the fun begin!

Sipping dew from a morning cup,
Little green jokers, never give up.
They tickle the air with laughter bright,
Throwing shade while basking in light.

A playful riot of color and cheer,
In their green world, there's no room for fear.
With a twist and a turn, they sing out loud,
In their own little jungle, they're fiercely proud!

Green Aspirations in Concrete Realms

In the cracks of stone, dreams arise,
Little green heroes, a clever surprise.
Against the gray, they stand with pride,
A funky parade, a leafy ride.

They poke their heads through asphalt dreams,
Turning sidewalks into funny themes.
Dancing hearts in urban spaces,
With joyful sprouts in strange places.

With every inch of stubborn might,
They wriggle and giggle, a quirky sight.
Creating pockets of life unfurled,
A bustling green in a concrete world.

So here's to the leaves with laughs so bright,
Challenging smog with all their might.
In every corner, they stake their claim,
Winking at overhead clouds, playing the game!

Nature's Promise in Every Leaf

In the garden, whispers sprout,
Each leaf a secret, a leafy shout.
They dance and twirl, a leafy ballet,
Promising sunshine will never decay.

When morning dew drops like a laugh,
Nature chuckles at our path.
Each petal a story, bold and bright,
Under the giggles of soft twilight.

Roots tickle the ground with glee,
Wiggling like worms at a picnic spree.
In every vein, a joke unfolds,
Nature's humor, timeless and bold.

So join the laughter, plants invite,
In their green world, everything feels right.
With every flutter, they sway and lift,
A leafy giggle, nature's gift.

Sunbeams and Leafy Idyls

Sunbeams tickle each sprouting leaf,
Making shadows dance, a playful thief.
In this leafy realm, laughter blooms,
As sunlight sneaks into garden rooms.

Playful breezes tease at the vines,
Whispering secrets like silly pines.
Little buds bounce in joyful cheer,
Singing a tune only the squirrels hear.

Leaves gossip about the rain's gossip,
As petals pirouette in a delightful skip.
The sun peeks through to join the parade,
In leafy idyls, laughter won't fade.

Frogs join in with a ribbit or two,
Joining the chorus, a leafy crew.
With every sunbeam that kisses the ground,
The garden chuckles with joy all around.

Flora's Expression of Time's Passage

In a world of greens, time hops and skips,
Every leaf is a page in nature's scripts.
Blushing blooms nod at the seasons in flight,
Singing of moments from morning till night.

A blink is a flower, a giggle a sprout,
In this lively garden, never a doubt.
Time trips through petals, with smiles to lend,
Poking fun at the past, our dear old friend.

With every bud burst, there's laughter to share,
Where time's a comedian, full of flair.
Leaves chuckle softly at memories past,
In the yard of giggles, time's shadows are cast.

So let's take a moment, to dance with the days,
And laugh with the flora in whimsical ways.
With nature's humor wrapped in each vein,
We celebrate time; it's never in vain!

Gardens of Light & Life

In gardens where giggles grow wild and free,
Light dances on leaves like a jolly marquee.
Every flower winks, it's a cheeky sprite,
In this leafy laughter, everything's bright.

Crickets strum tunes on a balmy eve,
Frogs croon in harmony, but don't be naïve.
The daisies gossip about gardening tales,
As the evening sun flips its happy sails.

Twirling petals invite the bees to play,
Butterflies flutter in their feathery ballet.
The daisies cackle, the roses join in,
In this light-filled garden, the fun won't thin.

So grab your hat and join the fray,
In gardens of laughter, come dance and sway.
For in each bright petal, there's joy to find,
Light and life embraced, all cleverly entwined.

Stirring the Soil of Potential

In pots we plant our hopes so bright,
With the sun as our guide, we take flight.
Leaves waving cheerfully in the breeze,
They chuckle and tease, oh what a tease!

Watering can, our magic wand,
Transforming dirt into something grand.
Roots stretching out, a little dance,
Who knew veggies had such a prance?

Soil's a party, with worms invited,
They wiggle around, so excited!
Sunshine beams down, a golden glow,
Even weeds, it seems, steal the show!

With dirt smudged smiles and muddy shoes,
We celebrate soil, it's what we chose.
For in this earth, potential thrives,
In a garden where laughter survives!

Green Horizons of Serendipity

Out in the garden, surprises await,
A sprout's got plans, it's feeling great.
One day it's tall, next day it's small,
Oh, what a ride, it's a leafball!

Nature's a prankster, never a bore,
A flower's a tease, opens one more.
Bees buzzing around, they join the fun,
Sipping nectar like they've just won!

A ladybug drops in for a chat,
Says, 'Life's too short to worry about that!'
Ants march on by in a funky line,
Dancing on leaves, oh so divine!

And who knew that dirt could be so chic?
With roots that groove and herbs that speak.
In this whimsical world of green delight,
Every day brings a new giggle or fright!

Nestled Dreams Amongst the Leaves

Under the canopy of leafy delight,
Dreams take flight, oh what a sight!
A squirrel does backflips, thinks it's a show,
While crickets chirp, they steal the glow!

Mushrooms peek out with a wink and grin,
Saying, 'Join the party, let's begin!'
They twirl in the shadows, all chummy and bright,
In their world, everything feels just right!

Sunshine splashes on patches of green,
Painting the world like an artist's dream.
Leaves whisper secrets, rustling away,
Nature's own chatter, holding sway.

Beneath leafy arms, we find cozy spots,
Where laughter bubbles and worries are knots.
Each bloom a story, each branch a song,
In this playful dance, we all belong!

Luminescent Whispers of Tomorrow

Stars twinkle down on our leafy friends,
Whispers of future that never ends.
With every petal that dreams to bloom,
A canvas of wishes fills up the room!

Fireflies dance with a flicker and flair,
Telling tales of the wonders we share.
In this night garden, giggles abound,
With every rustle, a joy is found.

The moon enters softly, a silver queen,
Illuminating hopes that glow in between.
Each leaf holds secrets, oh dear what fun,
They gossip and giggle till morning's begun!

Tomorrow awaits, with laughter in store,
A playful embrace that we all adore.
In the glow of the night, we'll plant our dreams,
Unraveling futures bursting at the seams!

Recital of Green and Growth

In the corner, a leaf took a bow,
Dancing softly, a plant on the prowl.
With a twist and a bend, it stole the show,
Who knew green could put on such a glow?

The sunlight chuckled, warm on the skin,
A worm wriggled by, grinning a grin.
Nature's recital, what a funny sight,
Plants in tuxedos, flaunting their might!

The pots held secrets, whispers of cheer,
While raindrops giggled, "We're glad to be here!"
Every leaf clapped, in synchronized glee,
Who knew foliage could have such a spree?

With roots tapping rhythms, a verdant band,
Soil was the stage, oh wasn't it grand!
Nature's own party, where laughter will bloom,
In the joy of the green, there's always room!

Threads of Botanical Continuance

A vine wove tales in spirals and loops,
Telling stories of sunlight and troops.
Leaves sparkled like pixels in a meme,
Nature's own chat room, or so it might seem.

Rooted in humor, the plants played a game,
'Who can grow fastest?' was their silly claim.
With watering cans filled, the drinks were served up,
A toast to the greenery! Cheers from each cup!

The daisies donned hats, and sunflowers grinned,
As the garden chuckled, no chance to rescind.
Each shoot reached for glory, each sprout had its say,
In the threads of their tales, no dullness today!

So here's to the garden, a riotous crew,
With plant parties raging, and gossip anew.
Nature's own sitcom, on repeat without end,
Where each leaf makes jokes, and all roots commend!

Where Dreams Meet Green Horizons

A plant in a pot dreamed of flying high,
With aspirations as vast as the sky.
It stretched out its leaves, hoping for flight,
While a ladybug laughed, "You'll take off tonight!"

The sun cheered it on, bright and so bold,
"Reach for the clouds, let your story unfold!"
Flowers blushed pink, as jokes started to bloom,
In a garden of giggles, dispelling all gloom.

Roots shared their gossip, in whispers so sly,
"Have you heard the news? You won't believe why!"
Each branch held its breath, in suspense and delight,
As dreams of the green took off into the night.

With stars in the sky, and leaves all aglow,
The garden kept giggling, putting on a show.
There's magic in dreams, where laughter will spring,
In a world draped in green, joy is the king!

The Language of Leaves Unfurled

In the garden, a leaf learned to speak,
With a rustle so soft, it felt quite unique.
"Hey there, my friend, wanna join in the fun?
Let's chat with the breeze, and soak up the sun!"

The petals replied with a flutter and sway,
"Of course, let's gossip, come join the bouquet!"
They shared all their secrets, from roots deep below,
The language of leaves, a conversational show.

A flower dropped jokes, with petals in tow,
As laughter took flight, like a butterfly's flow.
With humor exchanged, and rhymes all around,
The garden became the silliest ground.

So if you should wander through corridors green,
Listen close, my friend, to the fun to be seen.
In the language of leaves, each giggle and swirl,
Are the whispers of joy, in the world they unfurl!

In the Heart of Urban Green

In concrete jungles, secrets bloom,
Potted dreams chase away the gloom.
Leaves whisper tales with a twist of fate,
Urban dwellers, they navigate late.

Sunshine peeks through the office glare,
Plants giggle quietly, a breath of fresh air.
In every corner, a leafy surprise,
With little green fingers that wave from the skies.

Laughter sprouts where shadows might creep,
Jokes shared softly as moments we keep.
A fern in the hallway, a sapling in chat,
Nature's comedy, imagine that!

So here's to the greens that stand tall and bright,
They dance through our days and glow through the night.
In the urban sprawl, they give us the chance,
To chuckle and giggle, in leaf-laden dance.

Radiance Behind Leafy Veils

Behind the leaves, mischief does hide,
Curly wild vines are our garden pride.
They play peek-a-boo with the curious sun,
And hum little songs when the day's just begun.

In pots lined up like soldiers at ease,
They share punchlines that tickle the breeze.
The sunbeams poke through their leafy disguises,
To find hidden humor in garden surprises.

Plants plotting giggles, a whimsical spree,
In every green corner, a ruckus you'll see.
With roots in the ground and dreams in the skies,
They jest about growth and life's big surprise.

So raise up your glasses, let laughter be heard,
To the leafed-up shines and the jokes they've stirred.
In radiant greens where giggles entwine,
We find dreams and joys, forever divine.

Rebirth in Emerald Shadows

In the shadows green, a riot of fun,
Nature's own jester, cheeky and run.
Sprouts laugh and tumble, so cheerful, you see,
In the game of grow big, they're winning with glee.

Emerald laughter fills the bright air,
Witty and wise, those greens have flair.
Cleverly swaying, they weave and they sway,
Making up punchlines for a brighter day.

From pots to the garden, they giggle and weave,
Each twist and each turn, we're lucky to cleave.
Bouncing through seasons, with tales to abound,
These leafy comedians astound all around.

So toast to the greens, in shadows they play,
Rebirth with a chuckle, they brighten the fray.
In every nook where the sunlight does land,
They offer a wink and a fun leafy hand.

Echoes of Nature's Embrace

In every frond, laughter does bloom,
Echoes of joy carry in the room.
With humor and heart, they stretch and they sway,
Making us chuckle as they frolic and play.

The pots on the sill, a merry parade,
Dance to the rhythm of sunshine's cascade.
A chorus of green, with jests in their song,
Telling us patiently where we belong.

Roots buried deep, yet spirits so free,
They spin tales of wonder, as merry as can be.
From shadows they leap into glorious light,
Offering giggles with each leafy bite.

So heed the green whispers that bubble with cheer,
In the echoes of nature, let laughter be clear.
With each little leaf, an adventure awaits,
In the wonderful world that our humor creates.

Breezes of Hope Through Petals

In a pot so near the sun,
A plant sprouted, oh what fun!
With leaves that dance, they twirl and sway,
They laugh at clouds that come to play.

Winds whisper secrets, oh so light,
A comedy show, greens in flight.
The soil's rich humor, a fertile ground,
Nature's jokes, all around!

When branches bend, a little shout,
"Look at me! I'm growing out!"
With nature's gifts, we carve our way,
In this green world, we'll laugh and stay.

So raise a leaf, for all to see,
In every corner, glee shall be.
Together we bloom, with giggles bright,
In breezes of hope, we take delight.

Secrets in Botanical Dreams

In a garden where secrets dwell,
Plants gossip soft, with tales to tell.
A sunflower winks, the cactus grins,
A world of laughter, where joy begins.

With roots that tickle, no one would know,
How leaves share stories, high and low.
In whispers so sweet, they plot and scheme,
Creating a scene that feels like a dream.

When the moon paints silver on every sprout,
The night blooms chuckle, without a doubt.
With petals that dance like a playful breeze,
These botanical dreams are sure to please.

So let's join in, with a giggle or two,
In this leafy realm, where all is anew.
With secrets to share, both silly and grand,
In the garden of dreams, we firmly stand.

Tapestries of Evergreen Promises

Amid the foliage, bright and bold,
Lies a funny tale of greens retold.
Each leaf a laugh, each branch a jest,
In tapestries woven, nature's best.

Evergreen whispers as shadows play,
The sunlight tickles, come what may.
As roots intertwine, secrets unfold,
In this place, every tale is gold.

With ferns that flutter and ivy that climbs,
They groove to the rhythm of silly chimes.
Nature's encore, a leafy ballet,
In this vibrant tapestry, we'll sway and play.

So gather 'round, with glee in our hearts,
In the forest of giggles, where laughter starts.
With promises green, and joy so near,
We'll dance through the trees, spreading cheer.

Sprouts of Tomorrow's Light

In every corner of this bright space,
Sprouts of joy have found their place.
With tiny leaves that wink and tease,
They beckon us to laugh with ease.

The sunlight teases, a playful chase,
As seeds sprout forth, they start to race.
With roots that tickle and stems so spry,
In the garden of time, we can reach the sky.

The buds unfold in a classic prank,
As petals giggle, the colors crank.
Each bloom a clown, in the fixer's light,
A vibrant display, a colorful sight.

So let us follow where happiness leads,
In nature's embrace, we plant our seeds.
With sprouts of laughter and futures bright,
We'll dance through the day, in pure delight.

Colors Whispered Among the Green

In a pot where dreams ignite,
Leaves converse in hues so bright.
They tickle air with silly poses,
Dancing shy amidst their roses.

One leaf claims it's wearing red,
While others laugh, 'That's out of thread!'
A yellow friend with crooked spine,
Says, 'Blame the light, it's not the wine!'

Amidst this lively leafy jest,
The gardener's jargon is their best.
They share their sunlight-y tale with glee,
A hanging lamp is hanging—let it be!

Secrets of the soil's delight,
Whispered softly in the night.
With every giggle, twist and turn,
It's clear these greens are here to learn.

In the Shade of Aspiration

Underneath the leafy cheer,
Aspire to grow, but never fear.
Twists and turns, a little fun,
A leaf's got dreams just like the sun.

One says, 'I'll be a chandelier!'
Another, 'Me? I'm high fashion here!'
The pot rolls its eyes in delight,
Claiming a throne—it's quite a sight!

But soon they realize as they sway,
It's not the throne that makes their day.
It's laughter shared, along the stem,
In the shade they find their gem.

So they giggle as they grow tall,
In simple joys, they find the call.
Each leaf a friend, a silly muse,
Together in green, they can't lose!

Cradle of Nature and New Beginnings

In the cradle where roots entwine,
New buds whisper, 'It's almost time!'
With every twist under the sun,
They plot their journey just for fun.

'What's that? A breeze? A leaf parade!'
One brags, 'Oh, I'm the one who stayed!'
While another plans a daring leap,
To dance and sway, a promise to keep.

With every sprout, a giggle sings,
The joy of life that growing brings.
They sway and twirl, a leafy fling,
In the cradle of nature, let's share a swing!

Old leaves chuckle at the new,
'Just wait till you're in the dew!'
Every shake, every twist, a delight,
In this green wonder, they take flight.

Soft Movements of Leafy Enchantment

In the rhythm of a gentle sway,
Leaves embrace the light of day.
With laughter cradled in the breeze,
They chatter softly, 'Oh, such tease!'

One leaf whispers, 'I'm a little shy,'
While another winks, 'Stand up and try!'
They twirl and laugh, a leafy dance,
With every movement, they take a chance.

A gentle touch from the sun's fingers,
In this moment, pure joy lingers.
Leaves roll around with playful glee,
In their green world, they feel so free.

Together they sing a song of fun,
In this leafy realm, they've already won.
With every sway, a joyous shout,
In soft movements, there's no doubt!

The Art of Resilient Blooming

In the corner, leaves like sails,
Swaying softly through life's gales.
With smiles that stretch, oh what a sight,
They twirl with joy from day to night.

Pots on pedestals, quite the show,
Misfits in green, where sunshine flows.
Roots that dance, oh, what a cheer,
In quirky pots, we raise a beer.

Sunshine, water, with a wink,
They sip their drinks, don't even think.
Chasing warmth, they laugh and nod,
In harmony, they tease the sod.

In every nook, they take their stand,
Blurring lines of leaf and hand.
Oh, the laughter in the room,
Where green adventures always bloom.

Lush Stories Written in Green

In every leaf, a tale unfolds,
Whispers of sunshine and beads of gold.
Stretched like tales, they reach for sky,
Plotting their journeys, oh so spry.

Gossiping roots in the ground so deep,
Telling secrets, never to keep.
In pots together, they share a brew,
Complaints of soil, oh what's anew?

With spritz of water, they give a cheer,
Dancing lightly, shedding their fear.
While sunlight splashes, they sing in tune,
Jokingly promising to grow by noon.

In the nursery's warmth, they laugh and play,
Dreaming of gardens, come what may.
Twisted vines giggle, reaching for fame,
Oh, such a garden; who is to blame?

Where Nature and Dreams Collide

In the sunlight, dreams take flight,
Leaves with laughter, oh, what a sight.
They twirl and spin, the air is bright,
Nature's jesters in pure delight.

Clouds drift by, sharing secrets old,
Laughter ripples, brave and bold.
Roots hold fast, but spirits roam,
Up above, they find their home.

Dancing shadows on the floor,
They tap their toes, always wanting more.
In every breeze, a tickle, a tease,
Life's silly magic, it aims to please.

Here in chaos, with a wink and grin,
Each little sprout knows where to begin.
Nature and dreams, hand in hand,
Creating laughter across the land.

The Quiet Revolution of Leaves

Whispers of green in soft delight,
Rebels dancing in morning light.
With hearts of joy, they stand in line,
Plotting mischief, oh, what a sign!

They sway with purpose, oh so sly,
In unity, they wave goodbye.
Group hugs in green, a leafy brigade,
Shocking the world, a grand parade.

Each leaf a flag, each stem a vote,
In nature's beta, they gloat and gloat.
Raising their voices, true and clear,
They'll always giggle at our own fear.

Thus, in silence, revolutions grow,
In bright green colors, their dreams will flow.
Oh, the laughter that nature brings,
With every rustle, the forest sings.

Whispers of Verdant Dreams

In the kitchen, leaves conspiring,
Gossiping under the shining light.
They plan a party, oh what fun,
With tiny hats and tea so bright.

A cactus crashed, while trying to dance,
The ferns giggled, they took a chance.
With twists and twirls, they shook in glee,
Amidst the chaos, a party spree!

Petals curled in fits of joy,
A rogue vine stretched to play coy.
They laughed and spilled all their green tea spills,
In the wildest dreams, there's no time for chills.

So join the fun in this plant parade,
With leafy friends, let laughter cascade.
For every sprout bears secret schemes,
In whispering winds, fulfill our dreams!

Leaves That Speak in Silence

In a pot, a leaf gave a wink,
'Why are humans always on the brink?'
Chatting away, with clumsy pots,
They ponder life and all its thoughts.

A trailing vine went out for a stroll,
Wiggled its way to the garden's goal.
With perfect moves, it swayed with glee,
To show the world what it could be!

None could hear the leafy debate,
As branches chatted, it felt so great.
What secrets lie under the sun?
A world of plants, oh what fun!

So next time you water, take a pause,
Perhaps you'll hear their leafy applause.
With every sip, there's a story to tell,
In silent realms, they thrive so well!

Echoes of the Green Embrace

In the living room, a leafy cheer,
They throw a bash when you're not near.
A rubber plant floats on the breeze,
And the succulents giggle, if you please.

They swap their pots and trade their styles,
"Mine's got thorns, but yours reviles!"
The laughter echoes off the walls,
As tiny sprouts tell their leafy calls.

With undercurrents of mischief, oh my!
The orchids conspire to reach the sky.
They bounce and sway in harmony,
Celebrating their green journey so free!

And so we smile, as we peek inside,
At the party where plants never hide.
In every leaf, a joy untold,
In whispers of green, there's life to behold!

Beneath the Canopy of Tomorrow

Under the leaves, a meeting unfolds,
Where mossy men tell tales of old.
'What about watering?', asks a sprout,
And in unison, they all shout!

With giggles that rustle through the trees,
Petunias plot to catch a breeze.
While sunflowers stretch, reaching high,
Like a leafy choir, they aim for the sky.

The soil is warm, with laughter abound,
A symphony of greens in joyful sound.
Even the weeds want a chance to sing,
"Who knew this garden could be such a fling?"

So here's to the future, brightly in view,
With twinkling leaves and the sky so blue.
In every nook, dreams sprawl and bloom,
Beneath the canopy, there's always room!

Flora's Breath in Urban Air

In concrete jungles, plants wiggle,
Their leaves dance like they've found a giggle.
They sip on sunshine, a leafy spree,
Counting clouds like they're counting bees.

Pothos in the corner, with high hopes,
Dreaming of wild, free plant-based slopes.
Chlorophyll smiles paint the scene bright,
As ferns dress up for a wild night out right.

From window sills, they plot and scheme,
Budding aspirations, living the dream.
In every leaf, a story unfolds,
Of urban tales that are funny and bold.

They'll launch a green revolution soon,
With potted protests beneath the moon.
Swaying to rhythms of city buzz,
A foliage party, just because!

Beneath Emerald Horizons

Underneath clouds, plants ponder their fate,
"Will I reach greatness or just be late?"
Spindly stems stretch towards the sun,
Mimicking dreams of everyone.

Succulents roll their eyes at the rain,
"Who needs water? We're perfectly sane!"
With cacti jokes that prick the gloom,
Spikes and smiles fill up the room.

A dance party held on a sunny ledge,
With roots that groove and friends to hedge.
Petals whisper secrets, oh so sly,
Plant-based humor makes them all high.

As the day fades into leafy grace,
Each sprout takes a bow, proud of their space.
Underneath shooty stars they giggle,
Nature's crew knows how to wiggle!

The Language of Nature's Growth

In whispers of wind through the branches light,
Plants speak a language, it feels just right.
They share their gossip with tender roots,
And trade little secrets in leafy suits.

Petunias gossip with daisies in bloom,
While tulips send texts from their green-room.
They laugh at the sun, plotting a prank,
With shadows that shift on the garden bank.

Vines twist and twirl in a jubilant spin,
As nature's own dance scene begins to win.
"Let's grow taller, let's grow wide!"
They chant in rhythm, bursting with pride.

Each leaf a chapter in this green fable,
Creating stories that are truly stable.
In the heart of the garden, where humor's in tow,
Nature's laughter puts on quite the show!

Cultivating Tomorrow's Eden

In pots of dreams and soil of hopes,
Plants wink at each other, twisting their ropes.
"Tomorrow's Eden will be a blast,
With greenery popping up fast!"

They plot for growth in their leafy chats,
"Let's fashion a world that's fresh and sprat!"
From tiny seeds to daring sprouts,
Each plant knows what living's about.

As the sun dips low, they chuckle and sway,
Plant puns and humour light up the way.
Moments of joy in the warm afternoon,
Where even weeds join in the tune.

Digging deep for laughter, not sorrow,
Fertile soil of fun seeds tomorrow!
With roots intertwined in joy and glee,
This garden blooms with a promise of free.

Dreams Crafted in Green Embrace

In a pot, I found my fate,
With leaves that dance and sway,
I talk to them, they nod with grace,
Who knew they'd have such say?

A plant with dreams, so bold and bright,
It makes my morning cheer,
We giggle as we share the light,
A leafy friend so dear.

In sunlight's glow, we hatch a scheme,
To grow a garden wide,
With whispered hopes and silly dreams,
We'll take the world in stride.

So here's to leaves with vibrant zest,
Our laughter fills the air,
In every nook, we find our quest,
In every sprout, we share.

Luminescence in Nature's Keep

In a corner of my tiny room,
A plant shines like a star,
It stretches out to find some bloom,
And whispers, "Look how far!"

I water it with joy and glee,
It drinks like it's a champ,
In return, it jokes with me,
A leafy happy camp!

With every leaf, a laughter grows,
In shades of green so bright,
It plays the part of nature's prose,
Turning wrongs to rights.

So here's to friends with roots so deep,
In soil of dreams they lie,
Each day, new tales we gently sweep,
As nature's giggles fly.

The Journey of Green Growth

A tiny sprout beneath my care,
It pushes through the ground,
I cheer it on with joyful flair,
"What's that? Another round?"

Together we will climb the walls,
To dance upon the breeze,
Through ups and downs, through leaves that fall,
We'll savor nature's tease.

I whisper dreams, it sways with grace,
A duo, light and free,
In sunlit spots, we find our place,
And giggle endlessly.

In every inch it stretches wide,
We're laughing all the way,
My leafy friend, my greenish guide,
Will brighten every day.

Emerging from Shadows

In the dark corner, something stirs,
A plant with playful might,
Emerging slowly, leaves like furs,
It dances in the night.

With fingers green, I coax it out,
"Come join the sunny show!"
It stretches long, as if to shout,
"Let's steal the spotlight, go!"

In every poke of light it gleams,
I laugh and share a cheer,
For in this room, we share our dreams,
And banish all the fear.

So here's to life that breaks the mold,
With every sip of sun,
In leafy hearts, we find the bold,
And know that we have won.

Nature's Call

When morning breaks, my leaves awake,
They stretch and reach for more,
Each curl is like a tiny quake,
A call to life's grand tour.

I pour the water; they drink with glee,
A little party here,
With roots that giggle silently,
Their antics bring good cheer.

As sunlight pours, they bask and beam,
In nature's funny game,
Together, we craft magic's dream,
And learn to chase the same.

So let us all, both plant and man,
Embrace the silly day,
For nature's fun is part of the plan,
In green we laugh and play.

The Roots of Our Dreams

In shadows deep where roots reside,
They hold our dreams, they take their stride.
With quirky twists, they wriggle tight,
Sharing secrets in the night.

They dance below, they giggle loud,
Tickling thoughts, oh such a crowd!
While sipping dew from morning's cup,
They shout, 'Hey there, don't give up!'

Nurtured by our laughs and sighs,
These leafy pals in green disguise.
They plot and scheme for sunlight's grace,
And chase the bugs right out of place.

So let's rejoice, let's tap our toes,
As roots and dreams put on their shows.
In the soil of hopes so deep,
We'll claim the harvest, take the leap!

Green Dreams in Sunlit Corners

In corners bright, where sunlight beams,
Lie dreams so vivid, filled with schemes.
They stretch and yawn, they peer around,
And whisper secrets without a sound.

The leaves all giggle, a funny sight,
As they sunbathe, blissfully light.
With every breeze, they sway and hum,
'These green dreams know where the fun's begun!'

They count the clouds and play with rain,
Gossiping leaves, not a hint of pain.
Who needs a pillow, clouds will do,
To snuggle a dream, just me and you!

So if you catch a green delight,
In that warm corner, hold it tight.
For every laugh and tiny grin,
Brings your wild green dreams within!

Whispers of Leafy Promises

In leafy whispers, secrets grow,
Of joyous tales, they ebb and flow.
With every rustle, they spill the tea,
On what tomorrow might just be.

Winds carry laughter, tales abound,
In every rustling, joy is found.
From tiny sprouts to towering sights,
They brandish dreams on sunlit nights.

They prophesy in colors bright,
A quirky future, pure delight.
They bubble over with silly plans,
Dreams dressed up in leafy fans.

So listen close to what they say,
For leafy promises lead the way.
In giggles green, we find our fate,
Join the bubbling, don't be late!

Enchanted Growth Beneath Glass

Beneath the glass, where magic peeks,
Little greens play hide and seeks.
They stretch and bloom in playful twirls,
Curious friends in leafy swirls.

With every drop of morning dew,
They plot their stunts and dance anew.
In glassy realms of light and cheer,
They sing and sway, their futures clear.

With each new sprout, they laugh and tease,
In playful tones, they find their knees.
Twirling leaves with witty wit,
They giggle at the sun's warm hit.

So peek inside this green retreat,
Where charms and joys alike compete.
For enchanted growth is all around,
With every chuckle, dreams abound!

www.ingramcontent.com/pod-product-compliance
Lightning Source LLC
Chambersburg PA
CBHW070319120526
44590CB00017B/2738